# First World War
and Army of Occupation
## War Diary
France, Belgium and Germany

60 DIVISION
179 Infantry Brigade
Headquarters
4 February 1916 - 3 April 1916

WO95/3030/1

The Naval & Military Press Ltd
www.nmarchive.com
Published in association with The National Archives

Published by

## The Naval & Military Press Ltd

Unit 10 Ridgewood Industrial Park,

Uckfield, East Sussex,

TN22 5QE England

Tel: +44 (0) 1825 749494

www.naval-military-press.com

www.nmarchive.com

*This diary has been reprinted in facsimile from the original. Any imperfections are inevitably reproduced and the quality may fall short of modern type and cartographic standards.*

**© Crown Copyright**
**Images reproduced by permission of The National Archives, London, England, 2015.**

# Contents

| Document type | Place/Title | Date From | Date To |
|---|---|---|---|
| Heading | WO95/3030/1 | | |
| Heading | Bde Headquarters 1915 Feb & Mar 1915 Sep-1916 Nov | | |
| War Diary | | 04/02/1916 | 28/02/1916 |
| War Diary | | 01/03/1916 | 03/03/1916 |
| War Diary | Dorking | 05/03/1916 | 29/03/1916 |
| War Diary | Watford | 30/03/1916 | 03/04/1916 |
| Heading | 60 Division (formerly 2nd London Div) 179 INF Brigade HQ (formerly 2/4 London Bde) 1915 Feb & March And 1915 Sep-1916 May | | |

WO 95/3030/1

60TH DIVISION
179TH INFY BDE

BDE HEADQUARTERS
JLY — NOV 1916
1915 FEB + MAR
1915 SEP — 1916 NOV

60TH DIVISION
179TH INFY BDE

# WAR DIARY or INTELLIGENCE SUMMARY

Army Form C. 2118.

**2/4th London Inf Bde**    **Dorking**

| Place | Date | Hour | Summary of Events and Information | Remarks and references to Appendices |
|---|---|---|---|---|
| Dorking | February 4th 5th & 6th | | were entrenching. 2/15th Batt training | Weather bad. Fairly well done only. |
| | 8th | | Tactical Scheme of defence near Leigh. | |
| | 9th | | I lectured the Officers on above | Fair |
| | 9th & 2/15th | | Battalion drill | required a lot of instruction as regards fire discipline & passing of orders |
| | 11th | | 2/14 in Company attack on Headly Heath | |
| | 12th | | I turned out the troops at Alarm posts. | Scattered billets. I consider turn out |
| | 2/15th | | received the orders at 10.th & reported ready to march at 12.25 | Good |
| | 2/14th | | " " " 10.25 " " " " 11.25 | Fair Transport not ready |
| | 5/c | | " " " 10.20 " " " " 11.50 | Fair |
| | 4th Fd Ambulance | | " " " 10.27 " " " " 12.12 | Fair. I have issued orders on subject since to that next time there should be a great improvement |
| | 13th | 10 | Officers & 400 2/4 Lds B. went to Sandwich for Musketry Remainder of Battn exercised the Battn in attack on Headly Heath. | Weather bad. Very wet. |
| | 2/15th | | went to Reigate entrenching Continued | |
| | a | | A.O.Q & batts 2/14 U.B. went to Southampton for Overseas. | |
| | 2/14 | | 2/15th moved into billets Headquarters in London | |
| | 17th | | 2/13th & 2/16th moved from Maidstone to London. | I inspected the Headquarters, London & the Battalions did |
| | 22nd | | Inspected with G.O.C. the large drafts of 2/14th for Overseas | work marching in their recruiting area & drill in the parks |
| | 27th | | 2/15th returned to Dorking. | in London. |
| | 28th | | Companies in drill & Musketry drill. | |
| M.H. 1st 2nd 3rd | | | 2/16th arrived at Leatherhead | |

(Sd) E.O. Baird Colonel
Comdg 2/4th Ldn Inf Bde.

CONFIDENTIAL.

conf 55

Army Form C. 2118.

COPY OF
WAR DIARY  2/4th. London Inf. Brigade.
or
INTELLIGENCE SUMMARY.

(Erase heading not required.)

Instructions regarding War Diaries and Intelligence Summaries are contained in F. S. Regs., Part II. and the Staff Manual respectively. Title pages will be prepared in manuscript.

| Place | Date | Hour | Summary of Events and Information | Remarks and references to Appendices |
|---|---|---|---|---|
| DORKING. | March 5th. | | Tactical scheme of drill outposts 2/13th., 2/14th. 2/15th. the dispositions were fair and reports sent in by officers on the whole satisfactory. Some very good maps came in. | |
| | 8th. | | Inspected 2/15th. in bayonet fighting and 9th. 300 recruits from 3/14th. | |
| | 9th. | | Inspected 2/14th. in Extended Order.  Work only fair. | |
| | 10th. | | Inspected 2/13th. in drill outposts.  Work not accurate enough. | |
| | 11th. | | Heavy rain.  Battalions route marched. | |
| | 12th. | | Tactical scheme in attack & defence on Headley Heath. Thick fog which made communication difficult.  Fairly well done considering but all very slow. | |
| | 14th. | | Inspected kits of 2/14th. and 2/15th. | |
| | 15th. | | Saw 2/13th. in close order drill. Men steady but officers require much practice. | |
| | 17th. | | 2/13th. & 2/14th. in outpost duty.  Improving. | |
| | 18th. | | 2/15th. in attack.  19th. a blizzard. | |
| | 20th. | | Inspected the billets of 2/14th. & 2/15th.  Former badly kept and latter very clean & good. | |
| | 21st. | | Sunday Farewell Sermons preached congratulating the Battalions on their good behaviour. | |
| | 22nd. | | Tactical Scheme 2/13th. 3/14th. in attack: 2/15th. in defence. An instructive day and timing of attack good but a lot to learn yet. | |

Army Form C. 2118.

# WAR DIARY
## or
## INTELLIGENCE SUMMARY.
*(Erase heading not required.)*

Instructions regarding War Diaries and Intelligence Summaries are contained in F. S. Regs., Part II. and the Staff Manual respectively. Title pages will be prepared in manuscript.

| Place | Date | Hour | Summary of Events and Information | Remarks and references to Appendices |
|---|---|---|---|---|
| | March | | | |
| Dorking. | 23rd. | | Saw Battalions in close order drill. | |
| | 24th. | | Saw 2/13th. in Extended Order work. Extensions good but distances bad and orders not properly understood or carried out. | |
| | 25th. | | Battalion in advance & rear guard work. Reports sent in very fair. | |
| | 26th. | | Saw 2/14th. in attack which was not at all well done. | |
| | 27th & 28th. | | Preparations for moving to Watford. | |
| | 29th. | | 2/14th. & 2/15th. moved by rail to Watford. | |
| Watford. | 30th. | | 2/13th. moved by rail to Watford. | |
| | 31st. | | Battalions worked under the C.O.'s as the training areas are not yet available. I received a very complimentary letter from the Chairman of the Urban District Council, Dorking on the behaviour of the Troops while quartered there. | |
| | April | | | |
| | 3rd. | | Inspected the recruits arriving from 3/13th. Batt. from London. | |

(Sd. E.W.BAIRD,
Colonel,
Cmdg. 2/4th. London Infantry Brigade.

# 60 DIVISION
(FORMERLY 2ND LONDON DIV)

## 179 INF BRIGADE HQ
(FORMERLY 2/4 LONDON BDE)

1915. FEB. & MARCH
AND
1915 SEP — 1916 MAY

2902

www.ingramcontent.com/pod-product-compliance
Lightning Source LLC
Chambersburg PA
CBHW081517160426
43193CB00014B/2712